Fishing
for
Sunfish

by ROBERT BARTRAM

Have you always wanted to go fishing, but couldn't because there wasn't anybody around to show you how? You don't have to wait any longer. This book is as helpful a fishing companion as you'll ever need. Easy-to-follow instructions and dozens of detailed illustrations show you every basic step — from choosing bait and assembling equipment to locating, hooking, landing, cleaning, and cooking your catch.

Sunfish are the ideal beginner's fish. Catching them requires only simple, inexpensive, and readily available equipment. And, because sunnies are abundant throughout the United States, chances are there's a good supply of them in your local lake, pond, or stream.

So go on out and scare up some sunfish. And, if other fish come along to take your bait, don't be surprised. After all, they have no way of knowing that you're fishing for sunfish.

Fishing for Sunfish

ABOUT THE AUTHOR

Robert Bartram is an artist and angler whose interest in fishing goes back to his youth in Long Beach, California, where he used to cane pole fish for herring and opaleye perch from the lumber docks and the harbor breakwater rocks.

Fishing for Sunfish is the result of Mr. Bartram's many years of memorable fishing experiences with his son, John; experiences that began with teaching John to catch sunfish with a willow stick at the age of six. Besides fishing, Mr. Bartram's hobbies include fly tying and woodcarving. What does he carve? Animals and — naturally — fish!

Fishing for Sunfish
by ROBERT BARTRAM

J. B. Lippincott Company
Philadelphia and New York

U.S. Library of Congress Cataloging in Publication Data
Bartram, Robert.
Fishing for sunfish.
SUMMARY: Introduces the characteristics of sunfish
and gives detailed instructions on how to fish for them.
1. Sunfish fishing—Juvenile literature.
[1. Sunfishes. 2. Fishing] I. Title.
SH691.S76B37   799.1'7'58   76-41251
ISBN-0-397-31735-2

To JOHN

Sunfish are fun to catch and very good to eat. There may be a place near your home where you can catch them. They live in most freshwater lakes, ponds, and slow-moving rivers and streams throughout the United States.

Sunfish like quiet waters where there are lots of weeds, rocks, and fallen trees and branches to hide under.

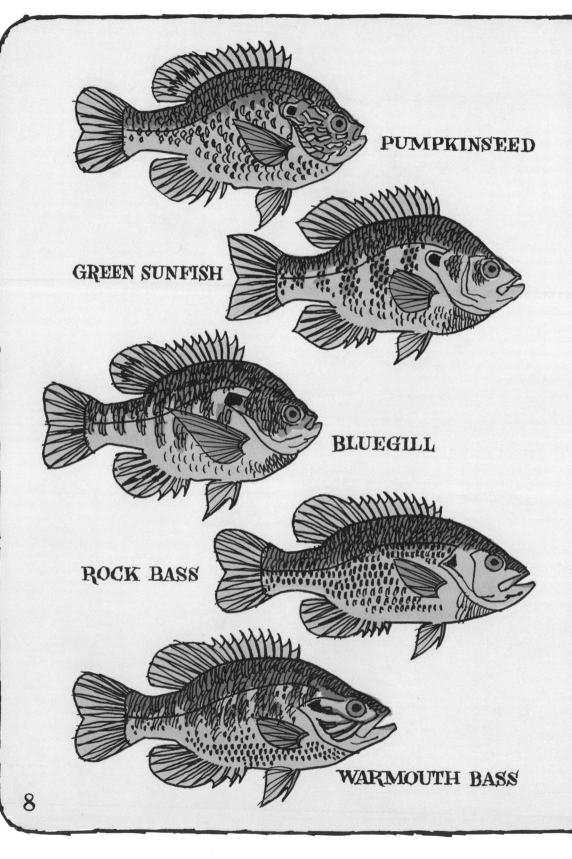

PUMPKINSEED

GREEN SUNFISH

BLUEGILL

ROCK BASS

WARMOUTH BASS

8

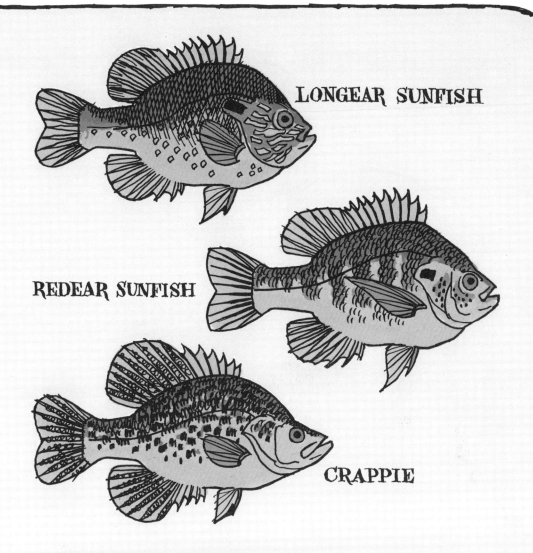

LONGEAR SUNFISH

REDEAR SUNFISH

CRAPPIE

There are many kinds of sunfish. Some kinds have different names. Here are some you may catch, depending on where you live in the United States. The map on the back cover of the book shows where the different kinds can be found. Sunfish are also called sunnies, bream, and panfish.

Sunfish are small; the largest ones usually aren't much bigger than your hand.

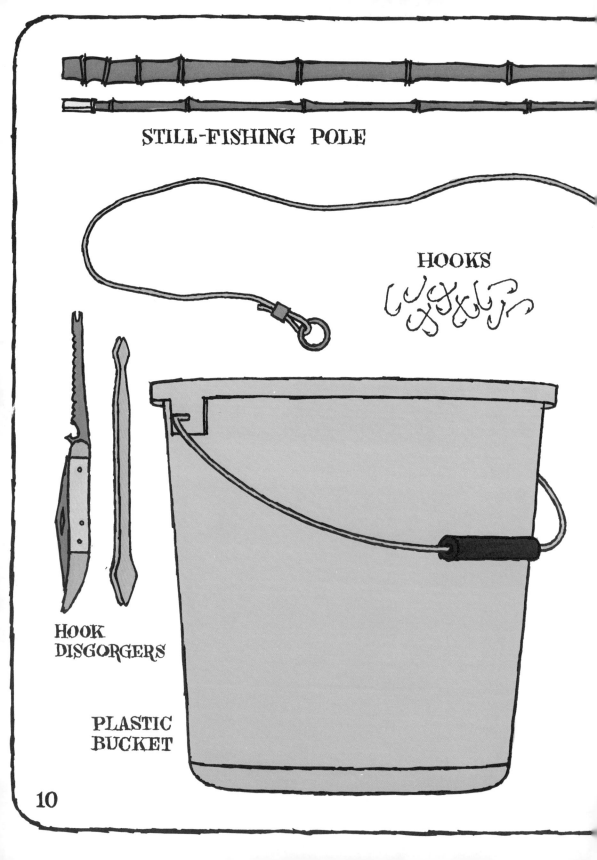

STILL-FISHING POLE

HOOKS

HOOK
DISGORGERS

PLASTIC
BUCKET

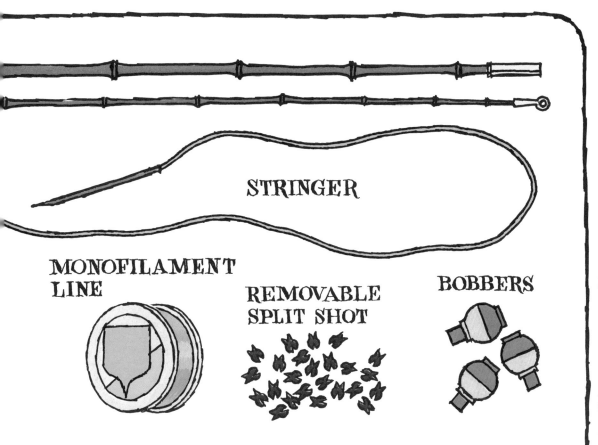

STRINGER

MONOFILAMENT LINE

REMOVABLE SPLIT SHOT

BOBBERS

You can learn to catch sunfish with simple equipment that costs very little. Most fishing tackle stores will have what you need. There are also mail-order tackle stores you can purchase equipment from.

Buy a two- or three-piece bamboo still-fishing pole and a spool of six-pound test monofilament line. (A "monofilament" line is made of a single strand. The "pound test" of a line tells you how much strain it can take without breaking.) You will need a dozen or so number eight hooks, a package of split shot, and a few small bobbers. You will also need a fish hook disgorger, a stringer to put your fish on, and a bucket to carry them home in.

Many kinds of live insects and worms are used as bait for sunfish. Earthworms are about the best. They can be bought at most fishing tackle and sporting goods stores. Or you may be able to dig your own. Earthworms will stay alive and healthy if they are kept cool and moist. At home, they can be kept alive in the refrigerator (not the freezer) for several weeks. Keep them in a closed container with some moist dirt in it. If you're fishing on a warm day, keep them out of the sun. Too much heat will kill them.

Sunfish have very small mouths, so small baits must be used. If you're using an earthworm, it should just cover the hook, with about half an inch dangling free. Cut large earthworms or nightcrawlers to the right size.

Artificial baits will fool sunfish sometimes. Try nature lures. These are made of soft plastic, molded in the shape of insects or worms. Small lures are best.

Plastic worms are made in many different sizes and colors. Buy the smallest size (two to three inches long). They can be cut shorter if smaller bait is needed. Put them on the hook just as you would live worms. Sunfish like most colors.

Artificial flies are made mostly of animal hair and feathers. Some are made to float. These are called dry flies. Others are made to sink. These are called wet flies. Size number ten or twelve flies are best for sunfish.

LIVE BAITS

NIGHT CRAWLER

GRASSHOPPER

EARTH WORM

CRICKET

COCKROACH

MEAL WORM

CATERPILLAR

HOW TO PUT THE WORM ON THE HOOK

This is how the worm should look on the hook. ➤

ARTIFICIAL BAITS

NATURE LURES

CRICKET

SPIDER

ANT

GRUB

PLASTIC WORM

A piece of plastic
worm on the hook.

ARTIFICIAL FLIES

DRY FLY

WET FLY

13

The best time to fish for sunnies is in spring and summer. They like warm water, and as the surface waters start becoming warmer, sunnies move into the shallows close to shore. This is when you can catch them with your bamboo pole outfit.

During the winter months, when surface waters become cold, and in some places freeze, sunfish move into deeper water where it is warmer. At this time they are not very active, and they eat very little.

Sunfish grow fastest in spring and summer. They become very active in the warmer waters, eating many kinds of insects and worms. Some kinds of sunfish also eat small minnows.

Aquatic insects live in the water. Many insects change from one form to another at different stages of growth. They hatch from eggs as immature forms called larvae. Then they change into adult forms with wings. Aquatic insects are food for sunnies at all stages. Sunnies find them in the mud and among rocks on the bottom, on the stems and leaves of water plants, and at the water's surface.

Terrestrial insects live outside the water. They become food for sunnies when they are blown or fall onto the water. Sometimes they are washed into the water by rains.

17

Each time you trim the line to put on a new hook, fly, or lure, the line will get a little shorter. When it gets too short, tie on a new line.

HOW TO PUT THE BOBBER ON THE LINE

Push in the spring plug to open the top hook. Put the line through the opening.

Release the plug to close the top hook on the line.

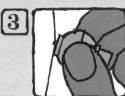

Slide the bobber to the distance you want it to be from the hook.

Hold down the top hook. Push in the plug so that the lower hook is opened. Put the line through the opening.

Release the plug. The bobber is now on the line and will not slide.

BOBBER AND WORM

SNAGGY BOTTOM

REMOVABLE SPLIT SHOT

Press here to put on.   Press here to remove

Split shot should be placed about a foot from the hook.

BOBBER AND FLY

DRY FLY

WET FLY

The bobber should be about two feet from the fly.

18

THE ANCHOR KNOT

Put the end of
the line through
the tip hole twice.

Bring the end
around the line and
through the loops.

Go around and
through again. Pull
tight and trim.

 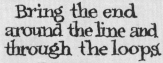 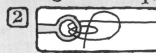

To rig up your pole, first tie the end of the monofilament line to the tip, using an anchor knot. The pictures show you how to do this. Then cut the line so that it is about a foot longer than the pole. A bobber or split shot can be attached to the line if needed.

A bobber adds weight to the line, making it easier to toss out your bait. Bobbers are used with artificial flies to help keep them floating or near the surface. With heavier baits such as earthworms and some nature lures, a bobber can be used to keep the bait far enough off the bottom so the hook doesn't get caught in branches or plants that may be there.

Split shot are small lead weights. You can add them if you want to keep the bait on or near the bottom. They also aid in tossing out the bait.

Often it works well to use heavier baits such as worms without a bobber or split shot, because the bait looks more natural and you can feel bites a little better.

19

HOW TO TIE A CLINCH KNOT

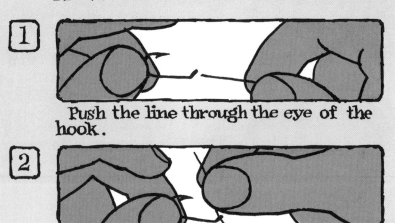

1 Push the line through the eye of the hook.

2 Slide the fingers of your right hand around the eye of the hook.

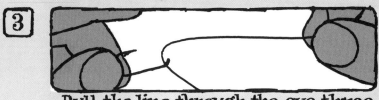

3 Pull the line through the eye three inches.

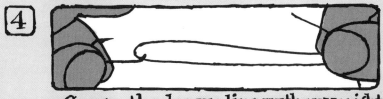

4 Grasp the lower line with your right hand.

The easiest way to tie the hook or fly to the line is with a clinch knot. It will be hard to do at first, but follow the steps shown and with some practice it will become easy. Different parts of a hook have names. It may be good to know them.

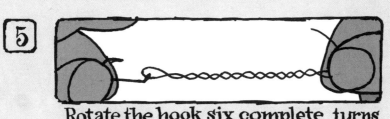

Rotate the hook six complete turns with your left hand.

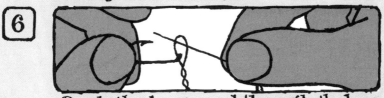

Push the loose end through the loop.

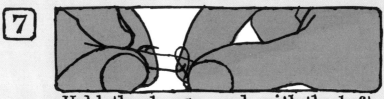

Hold the loose end with the left thumb and first finger.

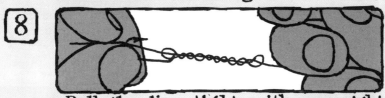

Pull the line tight with your right hand.

Nail clippers are good to trim the knot with.

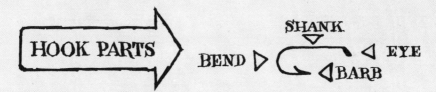

HOOK PARTS

SHANK

BEND ▷ ⊲ EYE ⊲ BARB

SHADY PLACES

FALLEN TREES AND BRANCHES

Part of learning to catch sunfish is finding them. Fish around weed beds, rocks, fallen trees and branches. Try under docks or overhanging trees and in other shady places. Sunnies usually gather in groups of twelve to fifteen. If you find a good place, you can catch several.

ROCKS

WEED BEDS

UNDER DOCKS

To find out which sunfish live in your state, match the black shapes next to each fish with the ones in the states.

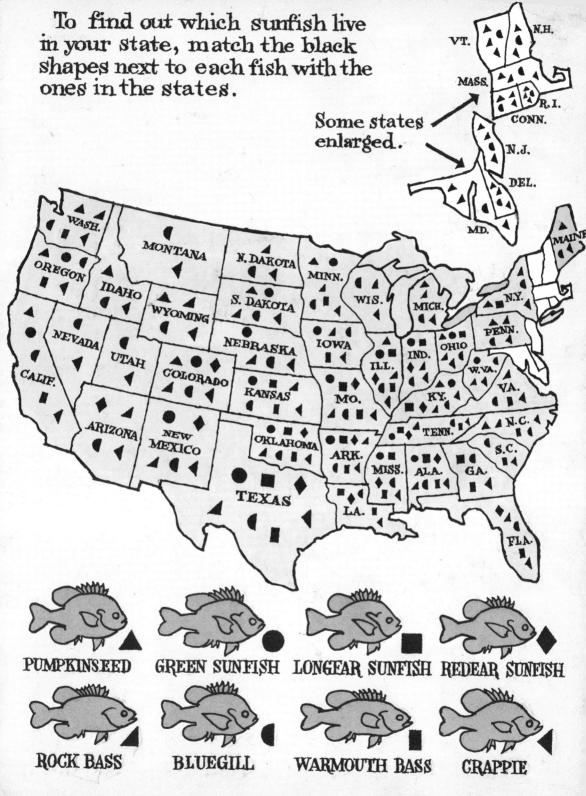

Some states enlarged.

PUMPKINSEED GREEN SUNFISH LONGEAR SUNFISH REDEAR SUNFISH

ROCK BASS BLUEGILL WARMOUTH BASS CRAPPIE

ISBN-0-397-31735-2

Sunfish scare easily, so approach likely-looking places quietly and without quick movements. Don't step on a fallen tree that goes into the water. Sunfish might be under the tree, and the sudden movement will scare them. They will be off to deep water, and it may be a long time before they come back. Even the movement of your shadow will scare them.

Toss your bait smoothly, so it falls lightly on the water; the louder the splash, the more it will scare the fish.

Sunfish don't like to move far from their hiding places, so toss your bait close to where they might be.

A strike may come right away, but usually the fish scare a bit and it may be several minutes before they will move toward your bait. Be very still and wait a few minutes. If you get no bites, start to bring in the bait very slowly. Try twitching the bait to make it look alive. A moving bait will often make the fish bite when a still bait will not.

Sunfish like different baits at different times. If you get no bites after a long time try another kind of bait.

When a sunfish sucks an insect that is on the surface of the water into its mouth, dimples and rings form on the water. These are easy to see when the water is calm. When you see rings, that's the time to try a dry fly and bobber.

Toss out the bobber and dry fly. Pull in the line gently so the bobber moves away from the fly but the fly itself doesn't move. Let it remain still for about thirty seconds. If nothing happens, try pulling in the bobber and fly slowly. Try the twitching movement so the fly looks like a live insect on the surface of the water. Sometimes a rapid movement works best. You can try this if a slow movement doesn't work.

When a dry fly has been used awhile, it gets soggy and begins to sink. Squeeze out the water between your fingers, then blow on the fly. Now it will float again. Sometimes sunnies will take a dry fly that has sunk. A wet fly may also work.

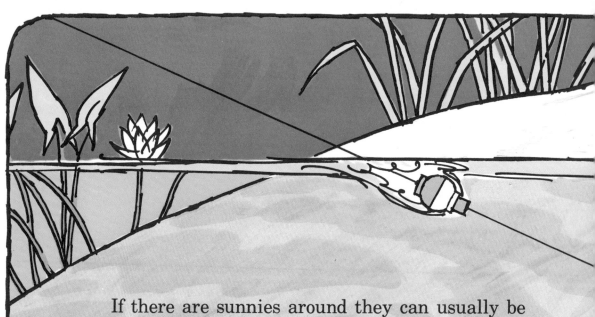

If there are sunnies around they can usually be caught with earthworms. When you feel a strong tug, it means a fish has the worm and is swimming away. If the fish feels too much resistance it will spit out the bait. Drop the tip of the pole to give slack line, wait a second, then hook the fish with a quick jerk. When you feel quick tugs the fish is only mouthing the worm. Don't jerk until you feel a strong tug. That's when the sunfish is taking all the bait and the hook into its mouth.

If you are using a dry fly with a bobber you will see the water dimple where the fish sucks in the fly. If you are fishing a sunken fly watch for the bobber to dip underwater. Sunnies will usually hook themselves on a fly, so you won't have to jerk hard to hook them.

When a bobber is used with a worm, the bobber will bounce if a fish starts nibbling. Wait for a strong tug that pulls the bobber all the way underwater before you set the hook.

BARBLESS HOOK

REGULAR HOOK
Barb bent down

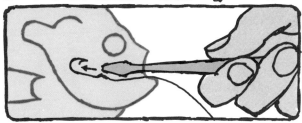

Fit the groove in the end of the disgorger into the bend of the hook. Push back to dislodge the hook.

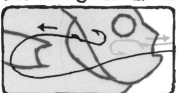

Pull the line through the gill opening and dislodge the hook. Then pull the line back out through the mouth.

Now you have your fish hooked. Don't pull too hard. If the sunfish is lightly hooked it could get free, so bring it in gently.

Sunfish have sharp spines in most of their fins, especially the ones on their backs. Be careful how you grab them.

As you bring the fish toward you, take hold of the line first. Rest the pole against your body so you have both hands free. Gently but firmly grip the fish, closing the fins and spines against the body. Now you can take out the hook and put the fish on the stringer.

When fish are caught with artificial flies they are usually only lip hooked, but if a fish is deeply hooked you may need a hook disgorger. A hook can sometimes be removed by reaching in through the gill cover. If the hook can't be removed, cut the line and tie on a new hook.

If you don't want to eat your catch you can use barbless hooks so the fish can be released unharmed. Barbless hooks can be bought, or make them by pinching down the barb of a regular hook with a pair of pliers.

Your catch should be kept as cool as possible. Put the fish on the stringer as you catch them, and keep them in the water. Tie the loose end of the stringer to a stick pushed into the ground, a tree root, or something else at the edge of the water.

Fish breathe with their gills and will not live out of water very long. Their gills cannot take oxygen out of the air as lungs do.

When you take the fish home in the bucket it's a good idea to cover them with moist leaves or grass to keep them cool. If you're going to be fishing far from home and it will be several hours before your catch can be refrigerated, take a cooler along with you. An inexpensive Styrofoam one will do. Put the fish in the cooler and cover them with ice so they will stay fresh on the trip home. This is very important in hot weather, when fish spoil quickly.

With sunfish, unlike many other fish, some states have no limit on how many you can take. If your state has no limit, it's all right to take as many as you can use. Sunfish multiply very fast, and if they get overcrowded there isn't enough food for each fish. Sunfish can even crowd out other kinds of fish. Fisheries and conservation departments encourage people to catch sunfish so the ones that are left can grow larger and so other kinds of fish have a better chance to grow and multiply.

SOME FISH ANATOMY

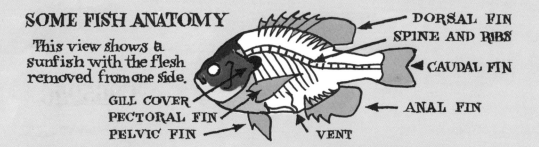

This view shows a sunfish with the flesh removed from one side.

DORSAL FIN
SPINE AND RIBS
CAUDAL FIN
ANAL FIN
GILL COVER
PECTORAL FIN
PELVIC FIN
VENT

Hold the fish by the gill cover. Scrape off the scales with a dull knife. Turn the fish over and scrape the scales off the other side.

The rest of the cleaning should be done with a sharp knife. Slit the belly from the vent to the pelvic fins.

It's best to clean your catch as soon as you can, because the entrails are the first part of the fish to spoil. Also, the scales come off more easily if you clean your catch right away. If you can't clean your fish outside, try not to make a mess in the kitchen. Put the sink strainer in the drain. Hold the fish down in the sink when scaling them so the scales won't scatter. After a fish is scaled, rinse it in cold water. The scales will collect in the drain strainer and can be removed. The rest of the cleaning can be done on several layers of spread-out newspaper. The heads, entrails, fins, and scales can be wrapped up and put in the garbage.

Make a slanting diagonal cut behind the gill cover and the pectoral and pelvic fins. Cut down in around the head to the spine. Turn the fish over and do the same thing on the other side.

Cut

Twist the head until the spine breaks. The head, entrails, pectoral and pelvic fins come off in one piece.

Hold the fish flat and cut along the top side of the dorsal fin. Press the knife blade down against the bones of the fin as you cut in. Do the same on the other side.

Cut around the anal fin the same way that you did around the dorsal fin.

To remove the fins. Grip the rear part with pliers and pull up and out. The fins and the fin bones will come out cleanly.

Rinse off your fish with cold water and they are ready for cooking.

Have a fish fry! Leave the tails on the fish; they make good handles. Dip the pieces in beaten egg, then in cracker meal. Fry the fish over medium heat in butter or oil until golden brown.

To eat them, hold by the tail and remove the meat from the back and rib bones with a knife or fork. A little lemon juice makes them extra good. Don't swallow any bones you can't chew up. They could become lodged in your throat.

Fishing for sunfish is lots of fun, especially when you know how to catch them. They are delicious to eat, and if you catch enough for a meal, you can treat your whole family to a tasty dinner.

A Rubber band can be used to hold the hook to the pole.

40